MW00710458

RODS
and CUSTOMS

Bo Bertilsson

MOTORBOOKS

First published in 2006 by Motorbooks, an imprint of MBI Publishing Company, Galtier Plaza, Suite 200, 380 Jackson Street, St. Paul, MN 55101-3885 USA

© Bo Bertilsson, 2006

All rights reserved. With the exception of quoting brief passages for the purposes of review, no part of this publication may be reproduced without prior written permission from the Publisher.

The information in this book is true and complete to the best of our knowledge. All recommendations are made without any guarantee on the part of the author or Publisher, who also disclaim any liability incurred in connection with the use of this data or specific details.

This publication has been prepared solely by MBI Publishing Company and is not approved or licensed by any other entity. We recognize that some words, model names, and designations mentioned herein are the property of the trademark holder. We use them for identification purposes only. This is not an official publication.

Motorbooks titles are also available at discounts in bulk quantity for industrial or sales-promotional use. For details write to Special Sales Manager at MBI Publishing Company, Galtier Plaza, Suite 200, 380 Jackson Street, St. Paul, MN 55101-3885 USA.

ISBN-13: 978-0-7603-2403-5
ISBN-10: 0-7603-2403-4

Editor: Amy Glaser
Designer: LeAnn Kuhlmann

Printed in China

On the front cover: (Top) Finally out in the sun, and it is where the Totte Landberg paint job looks its best. Totte started with a silver base, then silver Glowble, and tangerine candy on top. (Bottom) Rick likes the long lines of the chopped Pontiac, and Ken Ginnings did the custom bodywork on the car including rounding all corners on the doors and trunklid. The rear wheel fender openings were also modified and Ken made a pair of flush mounted fenderskirts

On the frontispiece: The old racecar-style included a set of Speedway Motors friction shocks in the front and the headlights are from a 1929 Model A with modern halogen inserts. The headlights were mounted extra low and out in front of the Model A grilleshell.

On the title page: The brand-new pickup bed is a lot shorter than a stock one, but it is built the same way. The tank is hidden under the bed and only the filler neck is sticking up.

On the back cover: (Top) John Brizio's 1934 roadster is all steel. Even if the body is a reproduction from Steve's Auto Restoration, it's as close as you can get to the real thing. Brizio's built the chassis on a set of boxed 1934 frame rails with a tube center crossmember. Brizio's is well known for building drivers that owners are happy to take for long drives. (Bottom) The profile of the Zephyr showes the streamlining that body man Ramsey Mosher created, with 8 inches of top chop, 6-inch extended rear denders, slimmed-down rocker panels, filled seams, and extended fender skirts. Ramsey also rounded all corners on the suicide doors, hood, and trunk.

Author Bio: Bo Bertilsson was born and raised in Stockholm, Sweden, and his interest for hot rods and customs started early. In 1969 he took his first trip to California to see the Grand National Roadster Show in Oakland. On this same visit, Bertilsson visited with Ed "Big Daddy" Roth. Roth wanted Bertilsson to photograph choppers for his *Choppers* magazine, and it was the beginning of Bertilsson's career as an automotive magazine photojournalist. He is now based in California and works for European publishing houses.

CONTENTS

FOREWORD BY ALEX XYDIAS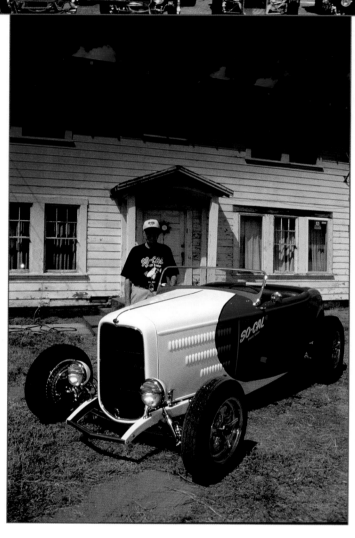

It seems to me that I have been asked the question of if I ever thought hot rodding would become as big as it is today a million times. Most of them already know the answer, and they just want to hear it from someone they consider a pioneer and who was lucky to grow up in the "old days" when it all started. A hot rodder before the term hot rod was ever born. Before I answer that question, let's go back to 1946 and see if you would have had the vision to predict the future.

When I opened the So-Cal Speed Shop in March 1946, the hot rodding activity in Southern California was limited, in most part, to hanging out at a few drive-ins, which usually resulted in late night street racing or running at the dry lakes. While all of that was fun, do you see a lot of future there? How about the "industry" that was making the parts I was selling in the shop? As the only employee at So-Cal, I had to drive all over town to pick up the stuff. I would go to Vic Edelbrock's on Highland Avenue in Hollywood. His "manufacturing facility" was two service bays in the back of a small gas station. Then I would go to Phil Weiand's over on San Fernando Road in Los Angeles. He worked out of a two-car garage in front of this mother's house. Next, I'd go over to Dean Moon's place in Santa Fe Springs. He had a small garage behind the family's café in the middle of an oil field. Can you see the future from there?

A young man named Robert "Pete" Petersen caught a glimpse of hot rodding's future and published the first issue of *Hot Rod* magazine in 1948.

From then on, hot rodding was a national pastime. Then came Bonneville, the NHRA, NSRA, Goodguys, and countless publications. Yet even at this point, it was still hard to predict the growth we have seen in the last decade and continue to see today. With his new book, Bo has shown us a bit of the history and many favorite hot rods and early customs. One of my favorite parts was checking out the flathead-T that he built, which tells the story of how many early hot rods looked like. An old time hot rod like that connects a lot to the early days of hot rodding, which is always nice to relive any day.

PREFACE

To write and take all the photos for a book like this can be a little like building a street rod. You have to collect the right parts, do the work, and polish it off before it is all done. In the end, it is a lot of fun work and very rewarding. For this book I have collected some of my favorite rods and customs from the United States and Scandinavia. I was born in Stockholm, Sweden, so I go there during the summer and cover some of the best rod and custom events. Hot rodding is big all over Europe, so there is no problem finding beautiful cars to photograph. You meet a lot of people at the events and photographing and writing features on specific cars for magazines and books. One person that got me on the right track early was Ed Roth. I first met him in the late 1960s and he was the person who got me started with photography because he wanted me to shoot some of the best Swedish bikes for his *Choppers* magazine he was running at that time. He sold the magazine before he got my pictures, but it got me started, and from then on I supplied the magazines with my features.

My personal favorites have always been hot rods and customs, which brought me on that first trip to California to visit the Oakland Grand National Roadster Show. That rainy winter day in Oakland, they had 300 roadsters in the show at the coliseum. I met Al Slonaker and he showed me around the show. It didn't take many years for my new hobby to become a full time job. After being part of the magazine business in Sweden, I moved to California and have worked for 16 years as a full time correspondent for some of the European magazines.

Through the years I've been in contact with most of the big name builders such as Roy Brizio,

Chip Foose, Roy Fjastad Jr, Pete Chapouris, and Terry Hegman, and have taken photographs of their creations. They have all given me plenty of help through the years and have made my work so much easier.

Another great aspect that comes with my work is the possibility to build project cars. The Flathead-T that is presented in chapter 2 was a lot of fun to put together. Finding the parts and learning about how the early hot rods were built was a very interesting history lesson for me. It also provided many new contacts, opened new doors, and provided many fun weekends. If you like hot rods and customs as much as I do, I hope you will have as much fun going through this book as I have had writing it and putting it together.

—Bo Bertilsson

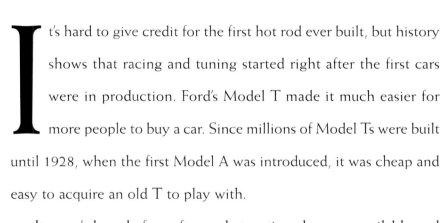

It's hard to give credit for the first hot rod ever built, but history shows that racing and tuning started right after the first cars were in production. Ford's Model T made it much easier for more people to buy a car. Since millions of Model Ts were built until 1928, when the first Model A was introduced, it was cheap and easy to acquire an old T to play with.

It wasn't long before aftermarket options became available and many cars were modified. The easy way to get a Model T into race mode was to unbolt all the unnecessary parts, such as fenders, head-lights, and windshield. People ran the dirt tracks with their race Ts, and pretty soon many wanted more horsepower. At this point, some started to make their own performance engine parts. The Model A and Model B engines made it even easier to get additional horsepower, so many racers used those engines in their Ts.

A 1932 frame will not follow an earlier T-Ford body shape at all, so Ron got some help from his pal Ray Carlson to do the frame and body modifications. The frame was shaped with the body hanging upside down, and the rails are now flat on top and shaped after the body.

Ron has been a hot rodder for the last 45 years. When he found this 1927 Ford Phaeton body for sale, he got the idea to build a classic-style tub on 1932 rails.

From the late 1930s on, we have much more information about when hot rodding started in a big way. The Model T became the car of choice for first-generation hot rodders, but soon they used the much stronger Model A frame under the old T-body, and later they used running gear, flathead V-8s, and so on. Even today, many hot rodders are going back to the early concepts and are building their cars using old ideas.

RON OLMSTEAD'S 1927 T-PHAETON

It's always hard to draw a line between street rods and real hot rods. In my eyes, the latter should be a car built with old Ford parts and stripped of everything unnecessary. Ron Olmstead's '27 Model T definitely fits that description. He started his project by taking a pair of 1932 Ford frame rails and the

four-seat T-body over to his friend Ray Carlson for modifications. These parts didn't fit together at all, but Ray hung the body upside down and modified the rails to fit.

When the frame rails were done, he used Model A crossmembers for the front and rear. The high Model A rear crossmember allowed clearance for the bigger Halibrand Quick Change. Olmstead used a 1936 Ford axle that was modified with modern 9-inch axles and brakes, plus the quick change V-8 center section, which was all completed by Wayne Atkinson in Indiana.

The front end was also built with old-style components, such as a dropped and filled I-beam axle, split 1932 wishbone, 1937 Ford spindles, and a Model A leaf spring. The brakes are from a 1948 Ford with Buick aluminum drums.

Many of us agree with Olmstead that the old 1950s and 1960s Buick Nailhead is among the best-looking V-8s you can drop in a hot rod. Ron found a good 1954 322-ci motor that was rebuilt but kept near stock, except for a Clay Smith 3/4 cam and a three-carb manifold. The perfectly red-painted Buick got a redrilled flywheel to fit a Chevy S-10 clutch and a five-speed S-10 transmission, which was bolted to the block with an adapter. The Nailhead motor gives Ron plenty of horsepower and bottom-end torque, plus the overdrive transmission drops the rpm to a much better level. With the quick change center sections, he can easily change the final gear.

Ray Carlson took care of the body modifications. Ford's Model T had a wooden frame that the body panels were nailed to. Carlson replaced the wood with steel tubing so he could weld all the body panels together. The 1932 grille shell was chopped 5 inches to better fit the lower T-body. When the basic bodywork was done, Olmstead took care of the finish work and then painted the car with black PPG paint.

After doing the wiring, Olmstead took the car to Dean Friend's Nostalgia Interiors. Friend stitched in the red vinyl upholstery over a pair of special seats.

Even if Olmstead lives in the hot desert, he'll often take his wife for a spin in the Phaeton. The Tourings and Phaetons are often given the nickname "tub"—as in bathtub—but who wouldn't like to drive a "tuned tub" like this one?

Above left: Ron wanted a classic hot rod motor, and when he found a 1954 322-ci Buick Nailhead, that was it. The motor, which was rebuilt and detailed, is close to stock except for a Clay Smith 3/4 cam and a Weiand manifold with three Carter carbs. The valve covers and plug covers are traditional Weiands.

Above: Ron swapped the original little flat dash for a cut-down 1932 dash that he filled with Classic Hot Rod Series gauges. The steering column is a 1936 Ford in combination with Porsche 914 joints and a Chevy Vega steering box; it also has a Bell-style four-spoke wheel on top. Dean Friend's Nostalgia Interiors stitched the interior in red vinyl.

Below: Wayne Atkinson rebuilt a 1936 Ford rear end with modern 9-inch axles, the later brakes, a Halibrand quick change center section, and an open drive line. The result is a modern rear end with an old-style Ford look.

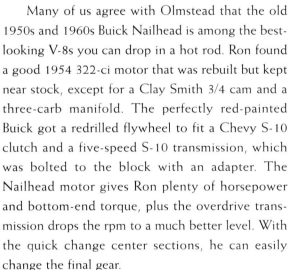

VON FRANCO'S TIME MACHINE

Ray Anderegg built this little roadster in the early 1950s from a 1927 Model T coupe. He couldn't find a good roadster body, so a cut-off coupe was the next choice. The body was channeled 4 inches over a home-built frame, the doors were welded shut, and the roof was cut off. The T-bucket-style frame with suicide front end had a basic flathead combination, a 1939 Ford transmission, and a 1941 Mercury rear end.

During the mid- and late 1950s, there were a lot of changes in the hot rod world, when many hot rods became race cars or show cars. In 1955, Anderegg entered the car in the Oakland Roadster Show. He didn't think he had any chance of winning the America's Most Beautiful Roadster Award, but he ended up in a tie with Blackie Gegeian and his black 1927 T for the big trophy. It became controversial because the Anderegg T was not a roadster, it was a cut-off coupe.

In the late 1950s, the car had a small-block Chevy with a three-carb manifold, a gold metallic paint job, and a white low hardtop. In this shape, the car was featured on the cover of *Hot Rod* (June 1957) and *Car Craft* (August 1959), plus many other publications. Then, like so many other hot rods from this time, it vanished.

When Von Franco was looking for something new to build and was going through old magazines for inspiration, the Anderegg T stuck in his mind. And the more he read about it—the award controversy and the fact that the car was gone—the more it became clear to him that it would be a perfect car to build.

Franco looked for the parts to build it in the later style, with the small-block Chevy, and talked to many of his friends about parts. First, he got "Taco" Bill Perea working on a 2x4-inch rectangular-tubing frame. The front end is based on a 4-inch dropped Magnum I-beam, with 1940 Ford spindles, Pete & Jake's hairpins, and 1940 Ford brakes. The

Ron used a set of early Ford 16x4-inch steel wheels with Firestone 4.75 tires in the front, and a set of 16x6 wheels in the rear with 7.00-wide Firestones. The wheels have chrome rings and Ford caps.

The little T looks great from the front, with its suicide front end, dropped magnum I-beam axle, chromed spring, and Pete & Jake's hairpins. The windshield Franco used on the cut-off-top roadster is a Model A type.

"Downtown Willy" in Torrance, California, did the interior in a white tuck and roll with purple piping and carpet. The dash was filled with a set of Moon gauges, and the steering wheel is from a 1950s Lincoln.

The T is not just a show car—
Franco and his wife, Katie,
drive it to some of the events
around L.A.

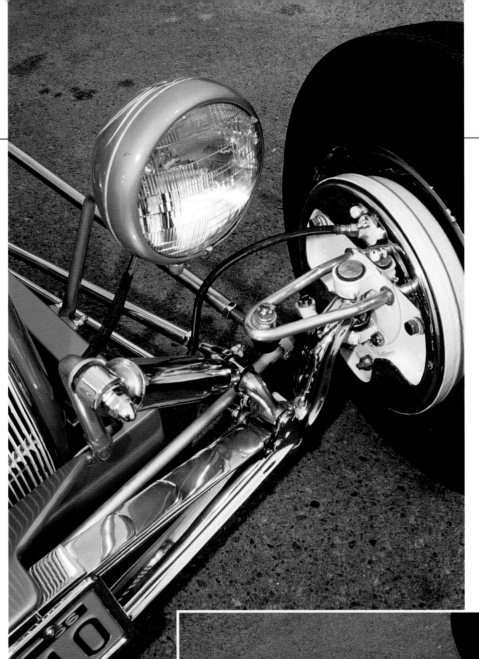

rear end is a 1957 Chevy with 1936 Ford wishbones and a 1940 Ford front spring.

Scott Craig rebuilt a 1971 350 Corvette motor, which was updated with an Offenhauser three-carburetor manifold with Rochester carbs. The motor was dropped in the chassis with a TH 350 transmission rebuilt by John Saltaman.

Franco was trying to recreate the old car's integrity, not just build a perfect clone. He got some help from House of Kolor to mix the gold metallic, and Craig Scott did the final bodywork and painting. "Downtown Willy," from Torrance, California, who did the interiors in the last few of Big Daddy Roth's cars, did the interior—white with purple piping and purple carpet, to get that 1950s style. The dash was fitted with a set of Moon gauges, and the steering wheel is out of a 1950s Lincoln.

The 4-inch dropped Magnum axle was combined with a set of 1939 Ford spindles and 1940 Ford hydraulic brakes. The brackets for Arrow headlights and the short, Pete & Jake's shocks were copied from the original Anderegg T.

Scott Craig rebuilt the 1971 Corvette 350 motor and topped it off with an Offenhauser manifold with three Rochester carburetors. A Walker radiator cools the white-painted Chevy, and the car has a set of chromed ramshorn exhaust manifolds.

Brackets for the steering box and pedals were the last to be welded to the frame, after we put the body on, so we could measure exactly where they should be welded. The steering box and column are from a 1937 Ford, and the pedal assembly and master cylinder are a mix of 1932, 1939, and 1940 Ford parts.

MOTOR AND TRANSMISSION

I bought a late-model flathead—a 1949–53 Mercury 110 horsepower—from Karl Jonasson, who saved it from the junkyard. It was lifted out of a pickup that was undergoing a complete modification at Boyd's. The motor ran well, so I kept it intact for the time being.

The transmission that came with the motor was a 1941 side shifter, but to save space in the little T, I used a 1939 transmission instead, which is a top shifter. Most hot rodders used the 1939 transmission for that reason, but it does require an adapter. This can be found on Mercury and Ford trucks—some are made of stamped steel and some are cast. I got the adapter with the motor and 1941 transmission, so I could just bolt the 1939 Ford transmisson to the flathead. A flathead just has to be dressed up, so I bolted on a pair of Edelbrock aluminum heads for some extra power, along with an Offenhauser two-carb manifold with rebuilt 97 Strombergs.

BODY AND DECK

I found the body at Specialty Ford Parts, and after asking Gene Scott about it plenty of times, he let me take it for $100. Even if it needed a lot of work, it was a stock, steel T-body. Later I found a door for it at Valley Ford Parts for $25. Now I just needed a good turtle deck.

I bought a fiberglass replica so that all the measurements could be taken. Some time later, I found a turtle deck for sale at the Model T swap meet in Long Beach for $70, and it was in pretty good shape.

Top: A new bracket was made for the 1937 Ford steering box, which was mounted on the side, to get the pitman arm on the outside of the frame. Specialty Cars made the pitman arm.

Above: With the pedal bracket welded to the frame, the 1939 Ford setup could be bolted to it with a 1946 Ford master cylinder. The brake lines are 1/4 inch, which was stock on '40 Fords.

The rolling chassis is together, and the 1935 Ford wire wheels had a set of Dunlop 5 1/4x16 tires mounted in the front and 7 1/2x16 Firestones in the rear. Orange County Plating powder coated the wheels before the tires were mounted.

Opposite: The 1922 Ford T-body was not in the best shape, and it doesn't look like much sitting there on the chassis. But it's an original body that can be rebuilt, and it gave me a much better feeling than a fiberglass replica.

To mount the body on the frame, I got a helping hand from Wolf Christiansson. He made a pair of sheet-metal channels that would cover the frame rails. With aircraft-type Clecos, I could then mount the channels to the body, and the body on the frame, before I took it to Klas Forsberg's shop in Huntington Beach where we got everything welded up.

Forsberg also made plenty of improvements to the body. He welded a piece of tubing to the upper edge of the body and then welded some square tubing around the door on the right side. Christiansson modified a Ford 1932 replica steel dash from Classic Manufacturing to fit the smaller T-body. Then I used an old-style insert from Lobeck Hot Rod Parts with a set of traditional Stewart Warner gauges from Hanline.

I chose to use weatherproof 1/2-inch plywood for the floor pieces, and Forsberg made the sheet-metal transmission hump on the floor, based on a full-size cardboard model I put together. Before the two pieces of sheetmetal were welded, I trimmed the hump, made sure it fit in the car, and had it fixed to a board with Clecos.

Right: The body was mounted to the frame with the help of sheetmetal channels and six 1/2-inch bolts. Wolf Christiansson did the sheetmetal pieces, which were later welded to the bottom of the body.

Below: To make the body rigid, Klas Forsberg used 1x1-inch tubing around the door. To make it even stronger, he connected the doorframe to the chassis with an extra bracket.

I found a pair of old-style "bomber-type" seats through my friend Conny Östlund, and Costa Mesa Auto Upholstery stitched up the cushions in black Naugahyde.

So-Cal Speed Engineering in Costa Mesa made the lake-style headers, and because they were local, Rick Carlyle could come over, measure, and do all the fitting right on the car. The rest of the exhaust system was done later by the local Mesa Muffler Shop, which included two Smitty mufflers.

The right style and size of wheels for a nostalgia rod are important. It's still possible to find the old stock Ford-style wire wheels. Kelsey-Hayes wire wheels are a little bit more expensive due to their bent-spoke style, and I liked the straight-spoke 1935 Ford style better. The front wheels are stock 4-inch wide, and Stockton Wheels widened the rear wheels to 5 1/2 inches. The front tires are 5 1/4x16 Dunlops, and the rears are 7.5x16 Firestones. With the bigger rear tires, the car has a little bit of a rake but you have to be careful and not change the height of the tires too much from the size it was built with. This would change the front-end angle, and you might end up with near-zero caster. The perfect angle would be close to 5 degrees.

For the floor, I used 1/2-inch, weatherproof plywood cut to fit between the channels. The transmission tunnel was created with some pieces of cardboard, then taken to Klas Forsberg, who made it from sheetmetal in two pieces. I trimmed the pieces to fit in the car and held everything in place with Clecos so Klas could do the final welding.

Right: You can still buy all the wood pieces for a Model T, so I replaced the door panels. After a few hours of work, the door looked like new.

The detail work will take nearly as much time as building the basic car and chassis. To make the wiring easier, I based it on a Haywire Nostalgia panel with all the wires marked.

It was a great feeling the day I fired up the old flathead and adjusted the ignition and carburetors. Not to mention the first test run around the block—that was a neat moment. It took more time than I thought to build the car, but most of it was spent getting all the parts together. I learned a lot about hot rod history during those years and managed to build it for less than $8,000, which might be hard to do today.

Next page: Dunlop 5 1/4 and Firestone 7 1/2 tires on 16-inch 1935 Ford wheels give the roadster a bit of a rake. The So-Cal Speed Engineering lake-style headers are chromed, and a 2-inch tubing exhaust system with dual Smithy's mufflers is hidden under the body.

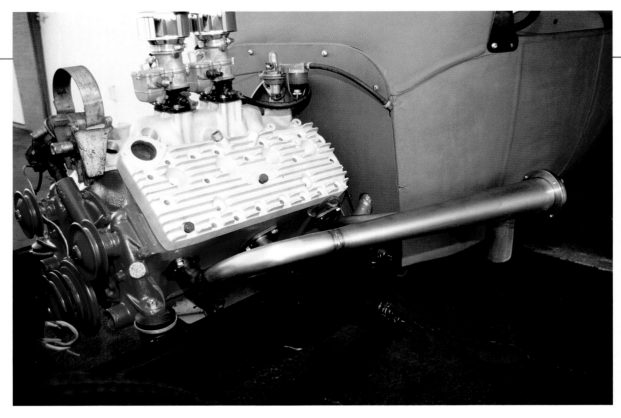

Rick Carlyle of So-Cal Speed Engineering came by to measure and make the headers for the roadster. After a few days, he checked the fit of the headers and it was perfect.

Left: Conny Östlund found the seats, which might be out of an English sports car or maybe even a World War II bomber. To add some comfort, Costa Mesa Auto Upholstery did the black upholstery on the seats.

Below: The fuse panel I used is Haywire's Nostalgia panel, mounted under the dash on a bracket to keep it away from the heat of the firewall. The Haywire wiring was all numbered, so it was easy to lay it out and get everything connected.

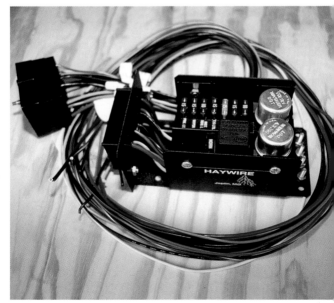

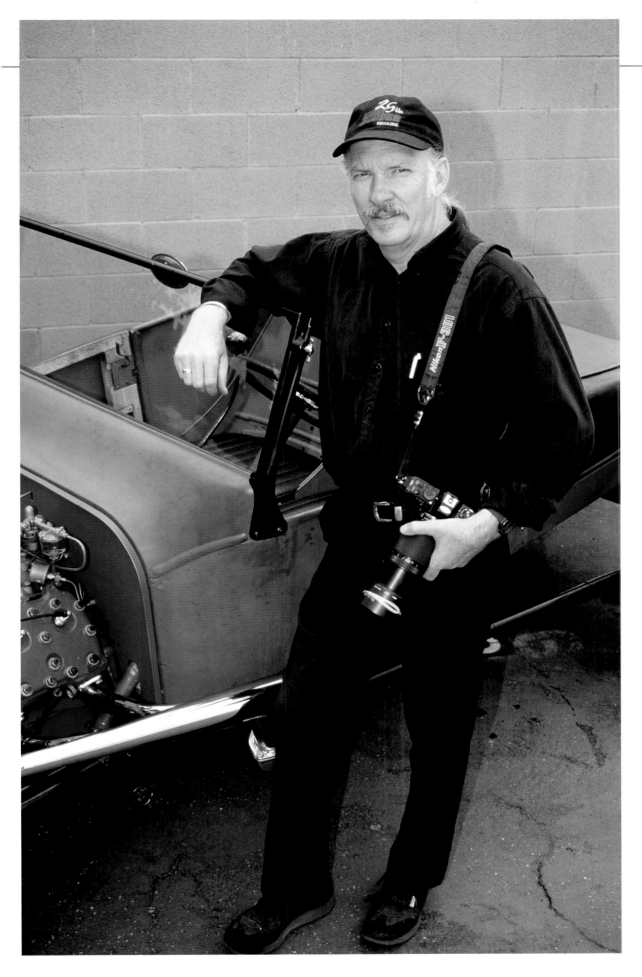

It's always a nice feeling to fire up the car and go for the first test spin around the block. In this case, the old Edelbrock heads leaked and blew out the head gaskets on the first few test runs, so I bolted the stock heads back on the Mercury motor.

CHAPTER THREE

Building a Model A has always been much less expensive than building the '32 and '34 Fords, but the A will also have a lower value in most cases. Many of the different Model A open bodies can be bought today as replica steel bodies, such as the 1928–31 roadsters and roadster pickups, which makes it a lot easier to build a neat street rod. The cost for those bodies is about 50 percent of what you have to pay for the 1932 replica roadster body, so for many hot rodders, it's still a much better alternative.

Starting with a brand-new steel body also means less bodywork and it cuts down the total cost of the car. However, you can still find plenty of original Model A bodies, and hot rodders will also use bodies that restorers have given up on.

To give the front end a clean look, make the new hood a little longer than stock and pinch in the 1932 frame to be cut and hidden behind the grille shell. The grille and grille shell are new replicas in steel.

The front end is 100 percent traditional, with a 3-inch dropped and drilled Model A axle that has 1939 Ford spindles, 1940 brakes, and 1958 Buick drums. Anders chromed all the possible pieces and painted the rest of it light green to match the dark, metallic green exterior.

The 1956 T-Bird Y-block 312-ci motor is nearly stock, but it has an Edelbrock manifold on top with three Ford carbs. A set of old Offenhauser valve covers also dresses it up.

temporary and covered with vinyl. The dash is filled with a set of Stewart Warner gauges, and Jeff made his own steering column plus the hub for the Lobeck steering wheel. A B&M shifter for the C6 transmission is on the floor.

We met Jeff on the white salt at Bonneville Salt Flats in Utah, where this roadster was one of the most photographed, cruising around between the pits and the starting line. On the way home from Bonneville, Jeff ran over something sharp and a tire exploded. Both Jeff and the car were okay, but it happened outside a little town in Nevada late at night, so it took him an extra day to get home. He did make it home, with some salt still on the car.

Y-BLOCK HIGHBOY

Anders Berge from Skepptuna, Sweden, had a '32 Ford earlier, but he wanted a classic nostalgia high-boy roadster. In order to get on the right track and find the parts, he called Micke Fors, who is "Mr. Nostalgia" of Sweden. He builds many of the nostalgia cars and is one of the best for finding parts. Micke helped Anders out by building the 1932 frame with Model A crossmembers in the front and rear. It still was going to be a little special because Anders planned to use a Ford Y-block motor and three-speed transmission. The goal was to build the car with 1950s and earlier parts only.

After Micke finished the frame with boxed rails and a new crossmember for the transmission,

A 1932 dash was filled with a set of old Stewart Warner gauges out of a '51 Scania-Vabis truck. The steering column and wheel came from a '57 Chrysler and were fitted to a '48 Ford pickup steering box. The shifter is for the '54 Ford three-speed transmission.

The rear wheels are 1950 Ford steelies, widened 1 inch, with 1946 Ford caps and 7.00 whitewall tires from Cooker.

Dave Gade did the interior in black and white Naugahyde. The steering column is a Mullen product with a Bell-type steering wheel on top. The steering box Paul used is out of a '28 Chevy. The 1932 dash came from Don Small and has a Stewart Warner insert filled with new Stewart Warner Wings gauges.

Opposite: A pair of original 1932 frame rails needed many long hours of filling holes and straightening before Paul took them to Norm Francis' jig. Norm used Model A crossmembers front and rear, then made a new tubing center crossmember. Don Small helped out with a 1932 wishbone and four Kelsey-Hayes wire wheels, widened and painted by Bill Winthers.

Anders took it home and started putting the pieces together. The front end he used has a 3-inch dropped Model A type axle, 1939 Ford spindles, 1940 Ford brakes, and 1958 Buick drums. The steering is based on a 1948 Ford pickup box with a 1957 Chrysler column and steering wheel. The rear end was a 1936 Ford axle with a Halibrand V-8 center section built by Micke Fors.

When Anders was ready with the brackets for motor and transmission, he took the 1956 T-Bird Y-block over to his friend Hasse Gyllensvärd, who rebuilt it while Anders was working on the rest of the chassis details. With the chassis rolling, the firewall of the 1928 body was bolted in place to make sure everything fit, such as steering, pedals, and brackets for the battery.

The roadster body was in pretty good shape when he bought it, so just a moderate number of hours were spent at the body shop before it was ready for paint. The two-color green combination with a white interior was right on. Just to be a little different, Anders had the painter do the 56Y lettering on the doors.

Anders took his time putting all the painted and plated pieces together before it was time to

Paul bought the 1940 Ford rear end from Les Delian and found the Halibrand quick change center section through a for sale sign on Norm Francis' wall. The 1940 axle tubings were cut and re-welded with 9-inch Ford ends. The brakes are drilled 1956 Ford F-100, and the high Model A leaf spring gives the Halibrand center section the space it needs.

take the roadster to Bilekipering in Stockholm for the final stage, the interior. A classic white-and-green tuck and roll was what he wanted, and Clas at Bilekipering didn't let him down. It came out of the shop just like Anders had hoped and gave the car that perfect late 1950s, early 1960s look.

With an Edelbrock manifold and three 94 carbs on top of the Y-block, plus a set of homemade stainless-steel headers, it was time for him to fire up his good-looking highboy. He took the hot rod meets by storm right away. Even if he didn't win Hot Rod of the Year, this might be the car that gives all the nostalgia rod builders a goal to aim for in Scandinavia.

DEAD RIGHT

When Paul Bos and his wife, Sallie, turned up at the Good Guys meet in Pomona, California, many of the top hot rod builders took a closer look at their new roadster pickup. Building a hot rod that will stand out in a crowd of thousands of street rods at the Good Guys event is not easy. Paul works as a heat-treating expert for a company in San Diego, and their hot rod takes most of his and his wife's free time. Both are always looking forward to taking it for a long drive to the weekend events between March and November.

While the new roadster pickup was built, Paul and Sallie drove their 1934 coupe. Two details

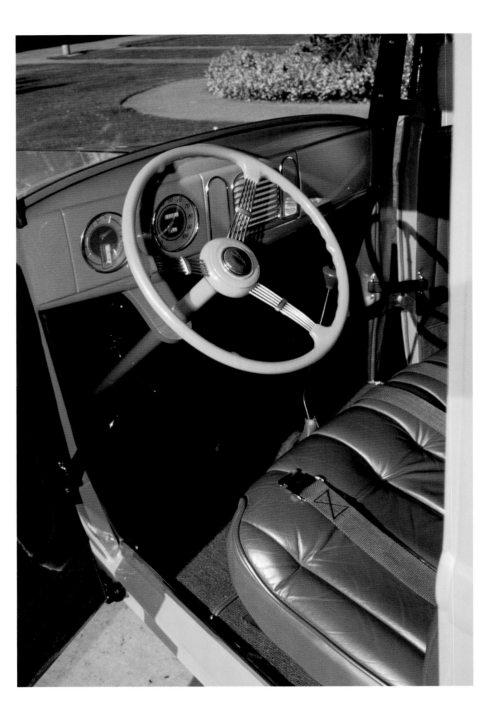

car even more class. The finishing touch was done right before my eyes when Rory the local pinstriper added the "Tommy the Greek" pinstriping. Jeff's restyled three-window is now ready to rock 'n' roll, and he just might start a new trend in Europe with this early 1960s-style hot rod.

JIM BENITEZ' 1932 TUDOR

Jim Benitez was born and raised in the San Diego area. He started working on hot rods when he was 13 years old, so he more or less has it in his blood. He has said, "I've always liked the 1930s Fords."

Even though Jim is only in his thirties, he built a bunch of cars before he started on the 1932. One day he ran into Larry Phillips, who wanted some

Above: The 1939 Ford dash needed plenty of modification before it fit the smaller 1932 Ford. Jim used the dash with the old gauges to give the interior a vintage style. The steering wheel is from a '36 Ford that has been cut down in size and hooked up to a '56 F-100 steering box.

Right: The headlights are rare E&Js from a 1927 Jordan. These lights are now popular with nostalgia hot rod builders. Some polish them, but others paint them in the exterior color. Jim made his own headlight brackets, which also support the shocks. You'll find a Matson radiator behind the replica grille.

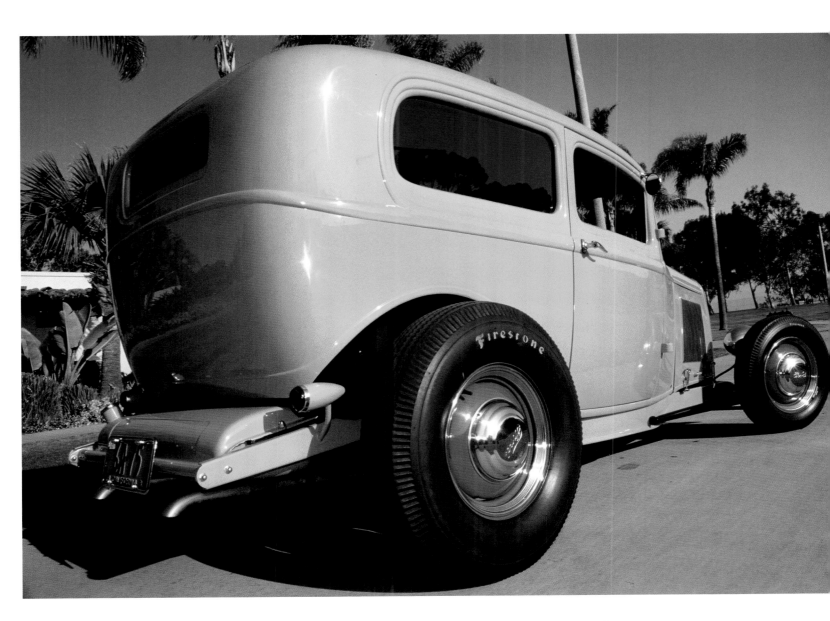

help with bodywork and paint on his '72 Chevy pickup. Jim knew that Larry had a pretty good '32 Ford Tudor sedan sitting in his backyard, so a deal was made. Jim got the Tudor as payment for the bodywork on the pickup. Jim was happy to spend some extra hours in the garage to build the hot rod he had dreamed about. His wife, Carrie, understood how much it meant to him, so she helped out as much as she could.

In 1998 he got the basket case home and started planning what to do with it. With the car

apart, Jim took the frame to Larry Phillips, who has a hot rod shop at home. Larry boxed the frame and got a new crossmember for the transmission.

Before the frame left Larry's shop, it had a dropped I-beam axle with split wishbone and a lowered leaf spring. The rear end is a 1972 Ford pickup 9-inch with 3.55:1 gears held in place by a homemade four-link and a pair of All American coil-over shocks.

When Jim got his chassis home, he could get things painted and put it back together. The Dago

The wheels Jim used are 1940 Ford 4x16 inch, with Firestone 5 1/2 tires in front and 7 1/2 in the rear to fit the car perfectly. The chocolate brown color on the wheels matches the interior as well.

The silver-painted 350 Chevy is from 1974. WAM in San Diego did all the machine work on it before Jim put it back together with 10:1 pistons and RV cam, along with an Edelbrock manifold and 600 Holley carb. A pair of blockhugger headers and 2-inch pipes take care of the exhaust.

The gas tank is an original 1932, mounted behind the body in the original place. The volume might be a little on the short side for long trips, but you can buy a replica tank today with a bigger volume.

dropped front axle got a set of 1940 Ford spindles, 1956 Ford pickup brakes, and Speedway shocks. The steering box is also from a 1956 F-100 pickup, and the column was cut together with a 1936 Ford column so he could use the 1936 Ford steering wheel.

The engine is a 1974 350 Chevy that WAM in San Diego bored and machined for him before putting it back together with new 10:1 pistons and a Chevy RV cam, which gives him some extra bottom end. The shop topped it off with a set of old 327 heads with 1.94/1.60 stainless valves. Between the heads, Jim used a Weiand manifold with a 600 Holley carb. Behind the engine, he bolted on a rebuilt 350 TH transmission that his friend John in Escondido did for him.

When Jim started on the bodywork, it was with a moderate chop of the roof. A 2 1/2-inch drop was just enough to still give him plenty of space. The body was in good shape, but he put in some hours to straighten it out before he took it to his workplace, All American Paint and Body, to do the last finish work.

When the body work was finished, it was painted in a special PPG color called Butterscotch that Jim and Carrie picked together. Jim had already painted the frame, so after about two years he got the chassis and car together for the final time. Then he and Carrie test-drove it for awhile before the interior was complete.

The dash is a cut-down 1939 Ford that nobody wanted, so Jim bought it cheap and made it fit the 1932. One neat thing is that he used the old gauges, and you wonder why nobody else thought about this combination earlier. The front seat is from a 1980s Toyota, which Jim and Larry modified for a better fit in the '32. Interior guy Frank Jacklone made the backseat before he upholstered everything in light brown leather.

When I first saw Jim's Tudor, it didn't have an interior, but to me it was a trendsetter and I had to get some pictures. For Jim, this has been the best work trade he's ever done. "Yeah, I did spend about $9,000 on the project, and today you won't find a good Tudor body for that kind of money, so I'm more than happy with it," Jim says with a big grin.

MR. NOSTALGIA'S ROADSTER

Micke Fors from Enköping, Sweden, has been seen in Northern European magazines for some time after building some neat nostalgia rods for friends and customers. Micke's latest rod is built with one of the new, replica steel bodies, and this time he built it for himself. He uses original Ford parts and early aftermarket parts for his cars, but it's getting harder to find them today since it is 50 years after they were popular. Through the years, Micke has

Micke's new 1932 roadster is very quick—he tested it at last summer's Swedish Hot Rod Reunion. The easy-revving 258-ci flathead has an extra-light bottom end, with Ross pistons (which are nearly half the normal weight), a Wilcap flywheel, and a Schiefer aluminum clutch. The big 31-inch Firestones and 3.78:1 gear combination helps, too.

Craig Neff's shop in Woodstock, Virginia. Craig sectioned the body 2 inches before he got started on the hand-formed front end in aluminum. Track-nose front ends are always critical to give the car the right look. If any of the lines are off, it could kill the look of the front end completely. Craig made not only the nose but also the rocker panels and rear pan. He also reshaped the cowl to fit a cut-down VW windshield and shaped the instrument panel.

Larry liked the old Moon/Potvin idea with a front-mounted GMC 6-71–type blower on a small-block Chevy. Besides the impressive look, it works well. The only problem with the setup is fitting it in a car. Saint Clare Engines in Memphis, Michigan, built the 350 Chevy. The short block was finished with a Crane cam and lifters for the special blower setup. Particularly with a blower, the heads become critical, so a set of late heads was fully ported, polished, and fitted with 1.94 size intake valves. On top of the motor you'll find a Holley 650 carburetor under the John West air cleaners.

With all the bodywork done, Russ Smith in Caro, Michigan, painted everything maroon. Then Bob King stitched the interior in beige leather over a set of new panels and two bucket seats.

Larry then took the car back to California, but this time he took it to Englishman John West in Costa Mesa, who took care of the final details. John did the grilles, both for the track nose and the rear radiator deck, the rear bumper, and many other changes to make it easier to drive. It took John about a year to get the car detailed and ready for driving. This 13-year hobby project is one of the best hot rods I've ever seen, and Larry is very happy with the finished car.

ERIK HANSSON'S B-400

Erik Hansson has built more 1932 chassis and put together more Brookville roadster bodies than

The chassis is all together and minutes away from Erik and friends lifting the body back on the frame. The trick 239-ci Ford flathead and the 1939 Ford transmission with Lincoln Zephyr gears are also in place. The rear end is a '36 Ford with a Halibrand quick change center section and a Model A rear spring.

After all the work was done, Erik put a for sale sign on the B-400 at the L.A. Roadster show in Pomona. It didn't take long before three guys were outbidding each other. No wonder Erik is smiling.

The stock dash was filled with a special set of Stewart Warner Wing gauges, and the 1940 Ford steering column is combined with an F-100 steering box. Erik used a restored '40 Ford Deluxe steering wheel on top of the column.

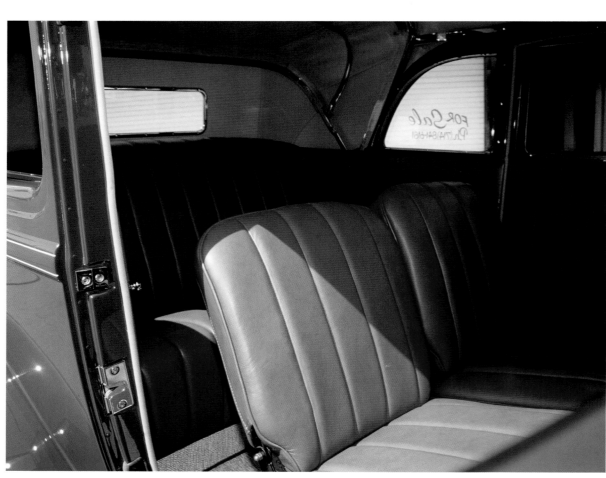

Fidde at Strömstad Bilinredning did the interior in brown leather over the stock 1932 Ford seats. A light beige carpet finished off the interior in a classy way.

anybody else in Europe, in addition to building many show winners and drivers during the last 25 years. Only a small number of B-400s were produced—about 800-plus cars—so they're not easy to find today.

In 1998, Erik got a hold of the body parts and started the restoration. It took parts from three different 1932s to fully restore the body. He had a good stock 1932 frame in the shop, which now was put to good use. This car was going to be a nice resto-rod, so he picked the parts carefully. He obtained most of them from swap meets and connections in the United States. Today it takes time and plenty of money to find the right parts for a 1932, but Erik was determined to get it done.

He also used all the chassis tricks he had learned through the years. The front end has a 4-inch dropped Mor-Drop axle with 1939 Ford spindles and 1946 Ford brakes. A stock wishbone and a spring with reversed eyes help the drop in the front too. Erik did some extra work and moved the rear crossmember a bit to get the rear wheels dead right in the rear wheel wells. The 1936 Ford rear end has a Model A rear spring to clear the Halibrand center section, but the crossmember is still the stock 1932 item.

Erik looked for a good, crack-free flathead motor for some time before he bought the 239-ci that's now in the car. The engine was a low-mileage military unit in perfect shape, so it only needed an Isky cam. He bolted on a set of Swedish-made Eelco twin replica heads and an Edelbrock Slingshot manifold with rebuilt dual 97 Stromberg carbs.

Behind the engine, Erik used a 1939 Ford transmission with Lincoln Zephyr gears. When it came to the brakes, he used 1946 Ford hydraulics all around and updated the stock pedals/mechanical brake brackets with a 1946 Ford master cylinder in a way that makes it look factory made.

After the body was lifted in place and the fenders were fitted, it was time to start the final finish

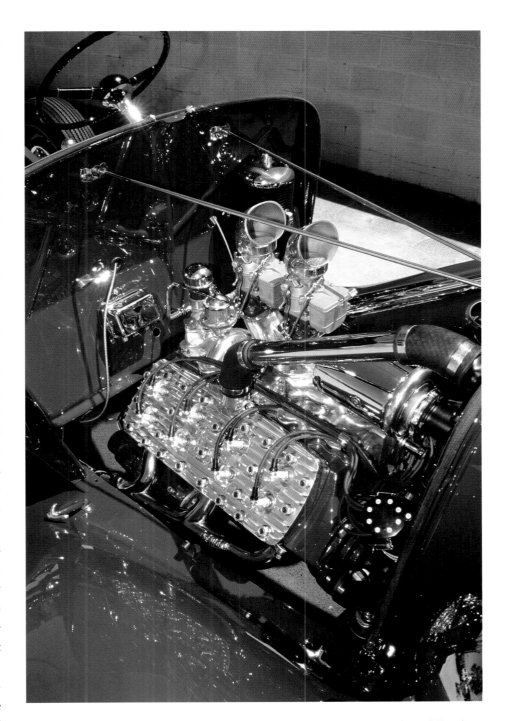

The Ford flathead was fitted with an Isky cam, Eelco dual-plug replica heads, and an Edelbrock Slingshot manifold with dual 97 Stromberg carburetors. The real trick part is the dual Vertex magneto setup, with a special front cover that came off a military tank flathead. The polished aluminum makes the engine look real pretty.

The body goes back on the chassis with the help of the boys from the Geoff Mitford-Taylor rod shop around the corner in Huntington Beach, where Erik and his Scandinavian Street Rods shop is located.

work. When he was happy with the fit of the doors and fenders, he took the car apart again to get it ready for paint. A friend in his hometown of Strömstad painted it old-style Ford Riviera blue. In the meantime, Fidde at Strömstad Bilinredning stitched the brown leather interior over a set of original 1932 Ford seats.

With all the pieces back at his shop, he had already started loading the container for the move to California. He quickly put together the B-400 and shipped it.

When he unloaded the container in Huntington Beach, the car didn't have a scratch on it. Yet he knew that to be really pleased with the result, he had to take the body off again and get the details finished the way he wanted. In a few weeks, the rolling chassis was finished and the detailing was perfect. He lifted the body on again and got the car together just in time for the L.A. Roadsters big event at Pomona. The B-400 was well received at the show, and there was a bidding war between three people for the car.

"CHOP-IT" 1932 PICKUP

Gary "Chop-It" Fioto heard the question from his wife many times through the years: "Honey, when are you going to finish that little pickup?" He knew that even if it took years, it would still be a very cool hot rod the day it was finished.

Gary has a custom car shop in Hicksville, New York, and has built all kinds of cars through the years. When he found the old '32 Ford pickup for sale in 1977, he had a vision of how it would look finished. Very low! As soon as he started measuring the truck, he knew that after a chop and a channeling job, the floor had to go. That meant that it at least had to be dropped down in the chassis to give him some legroom. So he named it "floorless," but he didn't start there.

The frame was boxed to begin with, and the crossmembers were custom made. The chassis is

It took Gary about 20 years to finish his dropped little hot rod truck, but the job was well done. He spent many hours getting the body just like he wanted it, and it took 6 inches of channeling, 8 inches of sectioning, and 7 inches of top chopping before it was "down."

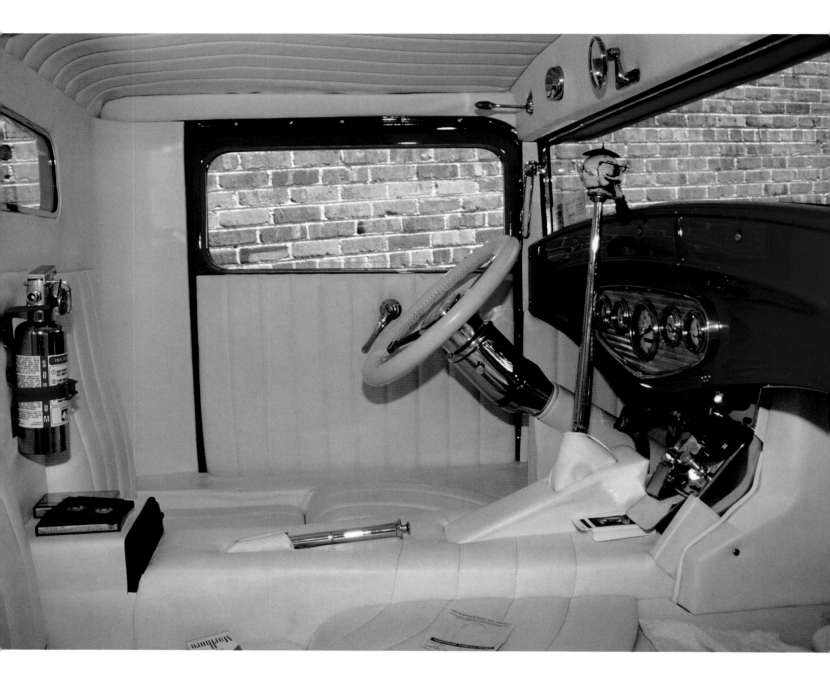

It took Gary some time to get the seat position right before he could get everything upholstered in white Naugahyde. The seats are lowered between the frame rails. The steering column, made by Ididit, is connected to a Corvair steering box.

pretty much a traditional hot rod chassis with a dropped I-beam axle, hairpins, and 1939 Ford spindles and brakes. The rear end is a 10-bolt Chevy out of a '65 Nova, which Gary installed with a set of four-bars, a Posey spring, and a pair of air shocks.

The plan also included a small-block Chevy with an Offenhauser six-carb manifold on top. The motor started out as a 1977 four-bolt 350 Chevy

and by the time it was ready to go in the truck, it had been rebuilt, detailed, and put together by Rob Rizzo. Gary dropped or channeled the body 6 inches over the frame, then cut out 8 inches in the middle to section it.

Now it started to get "down" to where he wanted it, but it was still too high on top, so he chopped it another 7 inches in the front and 6

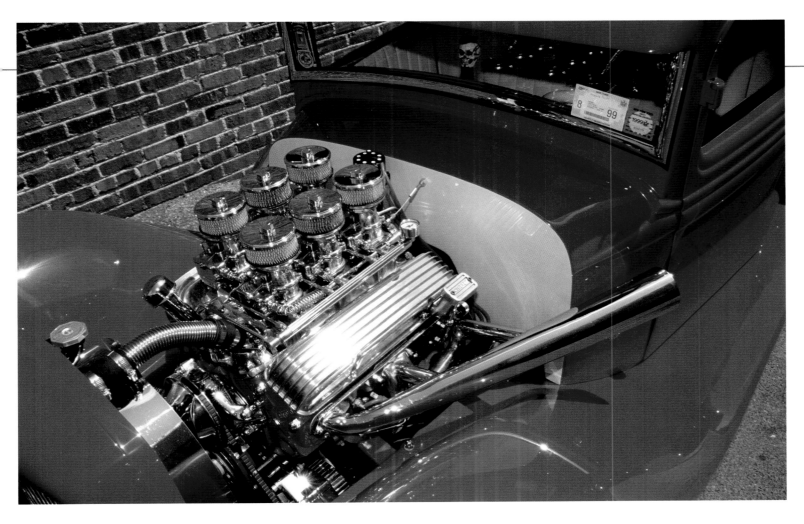

inches in the rear. In other words, getting the body right was a long process.

The fenders all around are stock 1932 Ford, and the grille shell in front of the new custom-built radiator is a cut-down 1932. Gary also did all the finish bodywork and painted the truck fire engine red. It took some time to get the seats done to provide a decent sitting position in the super-low pickup, but after that he had everything covered in white Naugahyde. In 1997, he rolled it out of the garage for the first test drive. Since then, he's taken it to shows all over the United States and has been winning plenty of trophies.

KEN CRITES' 1932 ROADSTER

This is an old family project, and Ken Crites of Huntington Beach has owned the car for the last 20 years. As a member of the *Outriders*, he also had an easier time finding the parts he needed. Twenty years ago when he first built the car, he used a Beverly Motor Cars 1932 frame with a full crossmember and made himself some modifications.

Top: The 350 Chevy looks pretty wild with the Offenhauser manifold on top and its six chromed 97 Stromberg carburetors, but it's pretty mild on the inside. Rob Rizzo built the motor and used a Crane cam, high-volume oil pump, and plenty of chrome pieces for nice detailing. The valve covers are 1960s Cal Customs.

Above: Just like in the front, Gary made a tube bumper for the rear and finished it with two pairs of 1959 Caddy bullet taillights. The *Beatnik* club plaque tells you he's a member of the famous custom club, which has members all over the United States.

The 2-inch chopped windshield is perfect for Ken and gives the profile a better overall look. Dennis Ricklefs did the "Tommy the Greek" pinstriping over the PPG yellow that Ken sprayed. To get the rake he wanted, the big-and-little combination in tires is 145s in front and 32-inch truck tires in the rear.

The 1948 Ford flathead motor was stroked with a Winfield crank and Mercury rods and pistons for 8:1 compression. Under the polished Eddie Meyer heads, you can also find a Winfield cam and Johnson hollow adjustable lifters. The manifold is a Weiand, with three 97 Stromberg carburetors. The cooling is taken care of by truck pumps, a Walker radiator, and an electric fan (just to be sure).

When it came time for the interior, Ken drove his roadster over to Jessie at Costa Mesa Auto Upholstery to get the light brown Naugahyde upholstery and the Wilton carpeting. Ken stuffed the dash with a set of Stewart Warner gauges in the SW insert and also hid a Sony stereo system with Boston speakers under the dash. The shifter is for the five-speed Chevy S-10 overdrive transmission, which makes the 3.78:1 gearing in the 1940 rear end a good cruising gear.

During the last rebuild, he modernized the drive-train a little to get a better final gear for easier cruising down the freeway. He modified the 1940 Ford rear end with modern 9-inch axles, Mustang drum brakes, and a set of Pete & Jake's ladder bars. The gearing he uses is 3.78:1, which is still a little bit of a high-rev gear for a flathead motor. Yet, with a late model Chevy S-10 five-speed transmission that has an overdrive gear, it gives Ken a perfect cruising speed.

When he built the motor, he started with a 1948 Ford 239-ci machined by Tim's Precision. A Winfield stroker crank in combination with Mercury rods and pistons give him 260 cubic inches. The short block was then finished off with a Winfield cam and a Melling oil pump. Ken also added a set of polished Eddie Meyer heads and a Weiand manifold with three 97 Stromberg carburetors.

The front suspension is based on an Okie Adams 4-inch dropped axle, with 1940 Ford spindles and 1940 Ford brakes with Buick drums. He uses a single front spring, shocks from Deuce Factory, and a set of homemade hairpins.

Ken did all the bodywork on the fiberglass replica body himself and also painted it PPG yellow. Then he called on Dennis Ricklefs to do the "Tommy the Greek" pinstriping in black and white. For the interior, Ken drove over to Costa Mesa Auto Upholstery, where Jessie stitched light brown Naugahyde upholstery over a custom seat done by Ken.

The roadster is driven every Saturday morning to the Donuts get-together in Huntington Beach and to many Southern California events and swap meets year-round, so this yellow flathead roadster is no trailer queen.

Ken modernized the old 1940 Ford rear end with Ford 9-inch axles and Mustang drum brakes, but it still has the old look. The rear spring is from the 1940 too, even if it was reshaped a little. The license plate says it all . . .

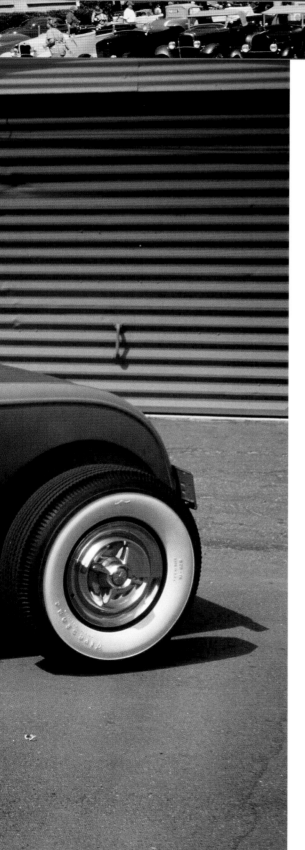

CHAPTER FIVE

T he younger generation of street rodders seems like a flashback to 40 years ago. Part of the problem with building hot rods today is that it's become pretty expensive, even if you use a fiberglass replica body. A lot of the original parts have become hard to find if you don't pay big money for them.

The new generation had a better idea to keep the budget down: build cars like the first hot rodders did. Instead of buying the dropped axles, chromed four-links, and expensive wheels, they build their own frame with the drop built in, use a stock early Ford suspension, junkyard motor, and so on. No fancy interior or paint job—just get it functional and have fun driving it. An old, rusty Model A body gets some new replica steel panels, and a cowl with doors becomes a roadster pickup body. In combination with the

To make the chassis older in style, custom hairpins by Deuce Frame were used front and rear. The rear end is a Currie 9-inch with Posies brackets and buggy spring. Front-end components are from TCI, Deuce Factory, and So-Cal Speed Shop.

homebuilt chassis, it'll be a neat little low hot rod. Model A coupes and sedan bodies are also among the favorites for these kinds of hot rods. Many of them are low with the body dropped over the frame.

ROB FORTIER'S 1929 ROADSTER

Rob started this roadster project after a visit to Verne Hammond of the Choppers club, who had a 1929 roadster body. He talked Verne into selling him the body and then got started on his new project. He wanted to use a stock 1932 chassis under the 1929 body, but after looking at a few he realized that cost

would be a big factor. Either the frame was really bad and too much work, or the owner was asking an arm and a leg for it.

Rob went to see Carl Fjastad at Deuce Frame in Stanton and they came up with a plan. A set of American Stamping frame rails, a 1932 front crossmember, a Posies rear A crossmember, and a tube center crossmember from Deuce Frame was what Rob needed. The pieces were put together in the chassis jig at Dagel's Street Rods. Rob also wanted the frame pinched to better fit the smaller 1929 body, so the frame now follows the body.

The project started when Rob saw the 1929 body at his friend Verne Hammond's place. Verne didn't really want to sell the body, but Rob talked him into it. Dagel's Street Rod's built the chassis with a set of American Stamping frame rails, Deuce Frame center crossmember, and a Posies rear buggy-spring crossmember.

The chassis was then completed with a traditional TCI I-beam front end, with Deuce Factory perches, shackles, and a Posies spring. The hairpins were custom made. Rear suspension was set up with a Currie 9-inch rear end and 3.50:1 gears, a Posies spring mounted with Pete & Jake's shocks, and a pair of hairpins.

While the chassis was being built, Rob had a 425-ci Buick motor and a TH 400 transmission rebuilt. Before the package was dropped into the chassis, Rob painted the motor in copper and detailed it with a set of polished aluminum valve covers and a Moon air cleaner.

Inside, a 1940 Ford Deluxe column is hooked up to a more modern and functional Flaming River Vega box. The spartan interior began as two pieces of plywood that Rob cut to fit the body. Then Rob drove his roadster down to Radi's Upholstery in Laguna and brought his favorite Mex blanket. Andy

The inside is still spartan, with a 1940 Deluxe steering column and wheel. No gauges? Well, there are two in the glove compartment of the 1940 Mercury dash. The seat was made from two pieces of plywood, some foam, and Rob's favorite baby blanket.

The Buick Nailhead is a big motor with 425 cubic inches, but it's small on the outside. There's plenty of torque and horsepower, so in a light roadster like Rob's 1929 highboy, it'll make the hot rod move. Rob detailed it with Moon valve covers; under the Moon air cleaner, there is a new 600-cfm Holley spreadbore carb.

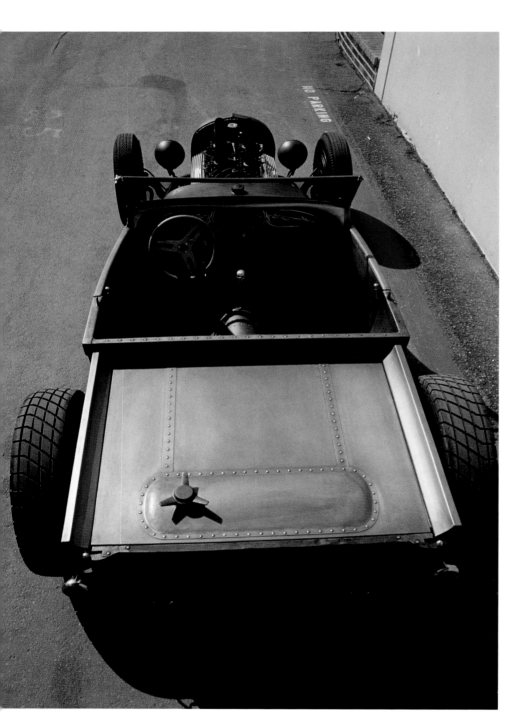

Jim Benitez from San Diego is featured with his yellow 1932 Tudor in chapter 4, but he's also started his own business. This is the first car built at his shop. The super-dropped roadster pickup is a work of art, built with a shipbuilding riveted style.

Radi made the seat with foam and stitched it up with the blanket so that Rob would feel right at home. The car was built in six or seven months, and even if it is still in a primitive stage, Rob has already had plenty of fun with it.

JIM BENITEZ' 1928 ROADSTER PICKUP

Some time after Jim finished his 1932 Tudor, he started to collect parts for a roadster pickup. He already had some parts in the garage and called around to get the rest of the stuff he needed. The frame got started with 2x4-inch profile tubing cut to create a 4-inch kickup in the front and an 18-inch kickup in the rear to get the car really low. When he got all the pieces welded together, he also put some extra time into getting Model A style on the frame horns.

Most of the front-end parts came from a '40 Ford, such as the spindles, brakes, wishbone, and steering box. Jim combined those parts with a new dropped I-beam axle and a single front spring. In the rear, he used a Chevy 10-bolt axle installed with a homemade four-link and a 1940 Ford rear spring.

While he was working on the chassis, his friend Buck Ronson in Ramona, California, rebuilt a good 327-ci Chevy motor for him. When Jim got the motor, he detailed it with an Offenhauser manifold and four Rochester carburetors, plus a pair of Edelbrock valve covers. Behind the motor, Jim used a standard Powerglide automatic.

When he lowered the body over the frame (4 inches), he started to think about maybe doing the bodywork a little differently. Why not do it all in bare metal and rivet all the pieces like a ship? With all the body panels ready, he riveted the body and the firewall together, and then also the rear of the body. The cut-down pickup bed had all the pieces riveted as well, and the new cover was going to really show off the riveted style, especially around the tank.

But what to do with the interior to stay with the rivet style? It had to follow the rest of the bodywork,

The interior is a big part of the design and rivet look of the car, so Jim hand-formed all of the sheetmetal to fit the look. The two little bucket seats might need some upholstery for longer runs, but the bare-metal look and the rivets are unique.

To keep things simple and on a budget, Jim had help from Buck Ronson to rebuild the 327 Chevy—which is stock, except for an RV cam. Jim detailed the motor with an unusual Offenhauser manifold and four Rochester carburetors. The headers were built with a Speedway Motors kit.

so Jim did the floor and driveshaft hump plus the two small bucket seats with rivets. It all looks like one-piece steel stamped out with a big press, and the rivets make it a work of art.

When Jim drove the car to the first event, Good Guys at Del Mar, it became a favorite of many right away. Jim won the Best Nostalgia Car Award the first day out, so he was very happy with the premiere.

The little 1929 roadster pickup became a favorite for many when it was first taken to the Good Guys event in Del Mar. Jim won Best Nostalgia Rod right away, so he was happy with the premiere, which also showed him that he was not alone in liking the car.

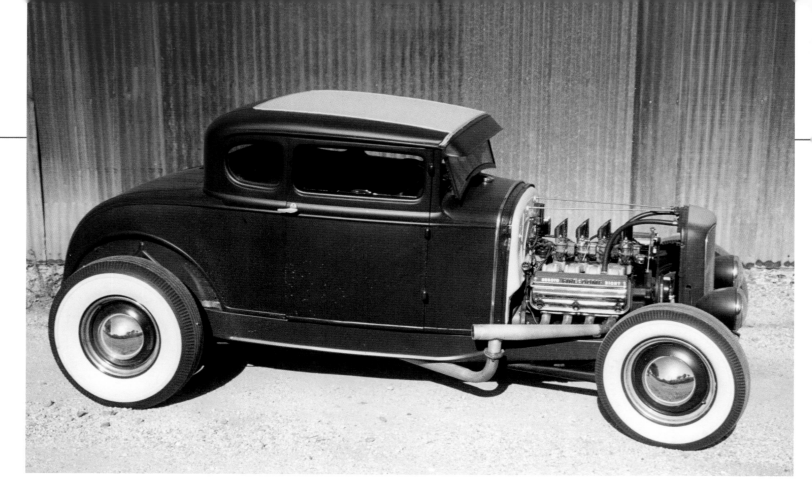

Lance Soliday bought his 1930 Ford coupe as a stock roller and then got to work and built a new chassis based on a 1932 frame with a 1934 center crossmember, Model A front crossmember, and a 1932 in the rear.

"CHOPPER LANCE" SOLIDAY'S 1930 FORD COUPE

Lance Soliday was inspired by Robert Williams' hot rod paintings for a long time, which made Lance become a hot rodder himself. Not just that, but he also started his own hot rod shop to help other rodders get their cars together.

As part of the *Choppers* club in Burbank, Lance also has his hobby and his own hot rod. In 1996, Lance purchased the 1930 Ford coupe for $2,500 and started working on it. The Model A frame is a little weak, and a 1932 frame would not only be stronger but would make a fenderless Model A coupe look much better. Lance found a set of 1932

The interior has been kept on the spartan side, with nearly no upholstery except for the seat. In old hot rod tradition, he used a 1940 Ford dash, which he got from his friend Verne. Some extra Stewart Warner gauges and a real 1940 Ford Deluxe steering wheel complete the interior.

The flat green paint, 16-inch steel wheels with wide whitewalls, and the radically chopped top just scream rockabilly hot rod. The headers with a couple of mufflers under the frame are also homemade, with a possibility of opening the headers for some strip action.

Below: Lance wanted a real hot rod motor in his hot rod, so when he found a 1953 DeSoto 276-ci hemi for sale, he knew it was perfect for the Model A. The motor was in good shape, so the only modifications were a Howard cam and a lighter Capanna flywheel. It was put back together with balancing, new rings, and new bearings. On top of the motor, Lance used a Weiand manifold with four 97 Stromberg carbs.

frame rails and used the Model A front crossmember, a 1934 Ford center crossmember, and a rear 1932 crossmember to get the frame together.

The rear end he used with the new chassis is a 9-inch, out of a 1958 Ford Ranchero, which he mounted with a set of Pete & Jake's ladder bars and a 1932 Ford rear spring. The front suspension was put together with a dropped Dago axle, the split 1930 Ford wishbone, and the 1930 Ford spring with reversed eyes. Lance used a 1939 Ford pedal setup with a 1940 Ford master cylinder for the hydraulic brakes. For the steering, he swapped the original 1930 box for a 1956 Ford F-100 steering box and he used the same column.

A unique feature of Chopper Lance's 1930 coupe is the choice of engine—in this case, a 1953 DeSoto 276-ci hemi. The engine is basically in stock shape, excluding a Howard cam and a lighter Capanna flywheel. With an old adapter, he bolted a GM four-speed behind the hemi and made his own brackets for the frame.

With the chassis ready, Lance bolted the body on to make some modifications. The big one was to chop the top 5 1/2 inches, which is a lot on any car. However, the Model A and earlier T are high in the roof, so the result was perfect. He also changed the stock dash for a 1940 Ford dash that

his friend Verne Hammond had. When he was pleased with the bodywork, he used a flat green paint that he sprayed himself.

He's kept the interior spartan so far and has been driving the car for a few years. The good news is that many of the new generation rockabilly hot rodders build their cars and do most of their own work, which gives hot rodding a chance to survive.

With the much shorter coupe top, which was also leaned at both ends toward the middle, it looks like a concept car of the late 1930s. Chip has an unreal eye for lines and details, which make his cars stand out. He worked closely with Doug during the years that he was doing the metalwork to make sure it would be perfect.

Steve Greninger made all the pieces that now cover the top of the LT4 Chevy engine, after Chip's detailed drawings. Everything is also functional, such as the small round door opening in the front for filling water. The engine is as clean as can be, detailed to the max by Andy Wallin.

The best guy in the business to do a grille for a street rod is Dan Fink, and his business just happens to be in the next block from Chip's in Huntington Beach, California. The grille is handmade in polished stainless steel and fitted in the grille shell Doug made. The headlights were made from 1939 Chevy buckets, then the two were cut and welded together. The chrome ring was also converted to one piece with a hidden fastener.

WES RYDELL'S 1935 CHEVY

When Wes Rydell from North Dakota asked Chip Foose and his team for help to get this project finished, they set a goal of the Detroit Autorama Show in February. Chip Foose had designed the car earlier, then chassis and body expert Doug Petersen built the chassis and did the bodywork. Doug had been working on the car on and off for about six years at his own shop before it was ready to be shipped to Chip's shop in Huntington Beach, California. You have to see a stock 1935 Chevy sedan to understand how much modification Doug did on the body. Chip had put every little detail on paper with drawings for his boys to work out from.

Everybody involved in the project knew that the judges at the Detroit show would check out every inch of the car when it was done. To give the body and the chassis a super fit, a special rotisserie was set up with the empty body and frame. This was to help the painter, Jason Mortenson, get a hairline fit between the two. More hours were spent finishing the body and fenders underneath than

ever before. When checking over the finished car, you cannot see any lines or wiring under it at all. Everything is hidden in a special tunnel in the body and on top of the motor.

Just the chassis, with the Bill Burbanea-built front suspension plus the Boyd-style IRS suspension with Corvette center section, plus all the detailing and special machine work, was more than enough to win some big awards. The brand-new, injected LT4 Chevy Corvette engine and TH

700R4 transmission were ground smooth, painted, and detailed to the max before the package was dropped into the chassis.

After the body was painted underneath and buffed out, it was time for all the interior and exterior detailing. The interior guy, Jim Griffin from Oregon, was ready early so he could get started on shaping the backseat and the headliner. Doug Petersen did the hand-formed dash for the special set of gauges, which were redone from the originals

The seats are highly modified, but Jim Griffin started with a pair of 1988 Jeep Grand Cherokee seats. Molds were made of the modified back panels and seats, then reproduced in carbon fiber before everything was upholstered in the light beige leather. Check out the seam in the seat that ends with the small Chevy bow tie emblems.

The wheels are a special Foose design: five-spoke 17-inch, in 7- and 10-inch widths. They were chrome plated after polishing, which makes it easier to keep them shiny. A mold was made for the center cap, with the Chevy emblem baked into it.

Right: Ron Whiteside has owned this 1934 three-window coupe since 1965, when he bought it for $150. The project got started around 1993, with a Hot Rods by Boyd chassis that Larry Sergejeff created with a set of extra-long SAC frame rails and a Boyd-style front and rear suspension.

with modern components. Dan Fink had already done the hand-formed billet grille.

Jason was under great pressure to do a perfect job painting the car in time for the show. Prepping and sanding took a lot of time. Chip and Jason tested out the colors to make sure they were getting exactly the right tone of silver and darker silver/green. With the painted body back on the chassis, the fenders were buffed underneath before being bolted back on the car.

The interior was coming together and Jim Griffin helped install all the pieces. The seats were modified 1988 Jeep Grand Cherokee. Jim made rear seat covers in carbon fiber before covering them in leather. It was critical that the headliner and window moldings fit perfectly.

Through the years, I have witnessed the construction of many best-ever-built Oakland Roadster Show winners, such as the Boyd cars. But this '35 Chevy had three or four times as many hours spent on the details, which makes it a real piece of art. Wes Rydell set his goal when he started this project—to build the best car he could. With the help

Chip Foose designed the long, low look, and with the chassis 2 inches longer, the wheelbase was stretched the same amount. Marcel's Auto Metal in Corona, California, did most of the body modifications including dropping the body over the frame; sectioning a piece out of the body/doors with more in front, less in the rear; and chopping the top.

As always, Chip got the best people in the business for his projects. When it comes to grilles, it is Dan Fink who makes super-nice ones—in this case, they are stainless steel and handmade. Steve Greninger, part of Chip's team of experts, made the headlights.

of Chip Foose, Doug Petersen, and the rest of the Foose team, Wes' goal became reality.

The car was just finished in time for the 2002 Detroit Autorama. The team had some nervous days before the 1935 Chevy was declared winner of the Riddler Award. Because it was also the 50th year for the Autorama, the big, prestigious trophy had a $50,000 check added to it.

RON WHITESIDE'S 1934 MERCURY COUPE

Ron Whiteside from Arizona has owned this 1934 three-window coupe for a long time, and he even used it as a drag race car in the late 1970s. He paid $150 for it, but that was in 1965. Ron wanted to

The LT4 Corvette motor is as detailed as anything else on the car. Steve made the cover over the fuel injection, while Andy and Karl detailed the engine to the max. For fun, Chip and Ron came up with the idea of putting Mercury emblems on the motor and calling the car a '34 Mercury, which makes a few people at the shows scratch their heads.

redo his 1934 completely and got Chip Foose to redesign it. At the time, Chip was the in-house designer at Hot Rods by Boyd.

Larry Sergejeff at Boyd's built a frame for it, making the chassis 2 inches longer and 3 inches narrower in the rear. The 1982 Corvette rear-end center section was completed with Boyd's axles, Carrera shocks, and Wilwood brakes. The front suspension is also a Larry/Boyd special with tubing A-arms, Fiat rack-and-pinion steering, Carrera shocks, and Wilwood brakes.

The project was put aside for a few years when Boyd's closed. It was taken to Chip when he opened his own shop in Huntington Beach. A new Corvette LT4 motor and 700 R4 transmission was dropped in. When it was time for the bodywork, it was taken to Marcel's Auto Metal in Corona. First the body was channeled over the frame and a new floor was made; then it was sectioned a few inches more in the front than the rear. The final cuts were done on top, which was chopped a few inches too.

A new hood and a slimmed down grille shell made the final lines come together. Chip's full team of experts worked full-time for eight or nine months to finish the car. After Steve, Doug, and Bryan were done with most of the detailed metalwork, the car

was blown apart and prepared for paint. This is a long process, especially if, like Ron, you want a show winner. Three months later, Andy, Karl, and Pete could start putting the chassis back together with everything painted, polished, and chromed. Every little thing was finished in the best possible way, so it was impressive to see the finished chassis with everything in place.

Interior expert Jim Griffin did the upholstery and hand-formed the seats before covering them with light tan leather with darker brown inserts. The headliner got suede, which made it unusual.

Fred hasn't had a chance to drive his new cars much yet, the speedometer only has a few miles on it after our photo session. The lines on the roadster that Chip Foose designed, Marcel's did the body for, and California Street Rods finished, are amazing. Not a single part on the car is from the original Ford roadster body.

Fred took the *ShockWave* all the way to Paul Atkins Interiors to get the Chip Foose-designed interior done. The center console was made first, then a pair of handbuilt seats; finally, everything was covered in the sand-colored soft leather.

Tom Morcotte and Chris Guinn painted the body underneath and the firewall, then rubbed it all out and polished it before the body was dropped back on the frame. After this, Andy, Karl, and Pete could start adding all the pre-made parts, such as the gas tank and steering column, and Pete could get the wiring done. Jim Griffin did the seats, door panels, and fit everything to make sure it was perfect before he did the final upholstery.

A brand-new Chevy LT4 Corvette motor was lifted into the chassis, then Andy Wallin detailed it with paint, chrome, and anodizing. Steve Greninger did the cover for the fuel injection, headers, and stainless-steel exhaust system.

The *AfterShock* coupe has the cleanest lines I have ever seen on a '33–'34 Ford Coupe, and the large Chip Foose–designed wheels give the car a special look.

Nick Perich stitched the interior over a set of aftermarket seats and a set of cardboard panels. The door panels were done with layers of plywood, then covered in the sand-colored leather.

Behind the handmade grille by Dan Fink, you can see the hidden Carrera coil-over shocks that are activated by a set of rocker arms.

With the body painted in Glasurit sedona fire, the rest of the detail work could be done while the painters finished the doors and fenders. It was a big moment when the car first rolled out in the bright California sunshine, and there was no doubt: this was not just Ron Whiteside's dream car, it was also the next big winner for the Foose design team.

FRED WARREN'S 1934 FORDS

It has always been a big goal for hot rod builders to win the Great Roadster Award at the Oakland Roadster Show, and today it takes a lot to win that trophy. You need a professionally designed and built roadster with thousands of man-hours by the best in the business. One guy who has all the right connections to create another big winner is Fred Warren from Warren, Ohio.

"Chip Foose designed it as a coupe for Chrysler to begin with but modified it to a roadster version for me. Chip has been a big part of the project, and even made a full-size wooden 'buck' for the people at Marcel's to have the exact shape of the body to work with," says Fred. The roadster got started during the last year Hot Rods by Boyd was open, and the Swede Larry Sergejeff built the chassis. He used

The dash got a cleanup, and all the extra holes were filled, but the gauge is from the stock '41 Ford, which has been given new chrome trim. The steering wheel is out of a '61 Caddy, which fits right into the Chip Foose-designed interior.

Chauvin Emmons did the 15-inch steel wheels for Squeegs and added 195 and 225/75/15 whitewall Diamondback tires. The front hubcaps are '57 Cadillacs.

In the late 1950s, Squeegs started playing around with candy paints, and through the years his special Gold Fire red candy has become a trademark. Squeegs' son Doug has learned most of his father's metalwork and paint tricks by working side by side with him.

Even if Squeegs tells everybody else to start a project with the best possible car, the 1941 was in pretty sad shape when he started. However, because it was a desert car it did not have any rust on it. Squeegs found the car in 1979 at the Las Tunas Indian reservation in New Mexico and trailered it home to Mesa. It sat behind the shop until about 1991. Then Squeegs got help from Butch Clark and Jim Moore to build the chassis.

They boxed the frame rails and Z'd the rear with a 6-inch drop. They mounted a Ford 9-inch rear end with a triangle four-link and an Air Ride Technologies setup so the ride height could be adjusted easily. They also added a Mustang II front-end crossmember with rack-and-pinion steering.

Squeegs dropped in a 1960s 428-ci big-block Ford, built and dynoed by M.A.C.H. After the chassis was rolled into the shop, Squeegs' friends helped lift the body on again.

M.A.C.H. rebuilt a late 1960s 428-inch Ford big-block motor and dynoed it to 440 horsepower before dropping it into the 1941 with a C6 transmission. The engine got a set of 9:1 TRW pistons, a high-lift cam, and ported heads. Between the heads, Squeegs used a rare 1961 406-ci tri-power manifold with a triple Holley setup under the aluminum air cleaner.

For a year and a half, Squeegs and Kenny Gatman worked intermittently on all the body modifications. They chopped the windshield 4 1/2 inches and tilted the posts back a few inches. They modified the complete front end with a longer hood, extended front fenders, frenched headlights, and added new grille openings. Squeegs also made the pieces for the grilles by hand. They rolled the lower edge of the rear fenders under, just like the front end, to give it a fully rounded look.

With the body ready for paint, there was no doubt about the color: it just had to be the Gold Fire special. This time it was not Squeegs who held the spray gun but his son Doug. He was proud to get the work done for his father and he sprayed the gold base with the red candy on top to get that special effect.

The interior was done in a 1950s and 1960s custom style, in white with a pair of 1964 T-Bird seats, a new wraparound back seat, and a center floor console. To finish off the project, Squeegs made a Carson-style top for it—first in Styrofoam, with a lot of cutting until he was happy with the shape. Then he made a fiberglass mold from it.

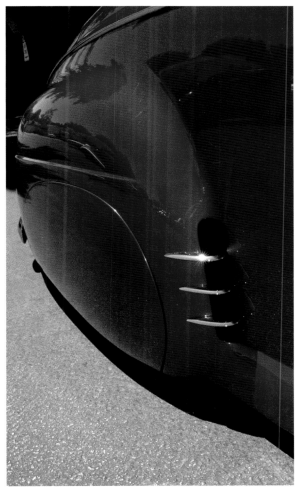

The details make the difference, and the scoops in the rear fenders, with the well-done chrome pieces, show how Squeegs planned everything. The lower edge of the fenders got a roll-under extension to make the lines perfect.

Scott wanted his '46 Tudor extra low in front, and the car already had a Heidt/Mustang II front end, so he installed dropped TCI spindles and cut the springs a bit. The front brakes are 11-inch Ford discs, with Granada (U.S.) calipers inside the painted 5x15-inch Wheelsmith steel wheels with 1948 caps.

Above: Susie Q, bass player for the Hot Rod Trio, relaxes with an old-fashioned ice cream during Friday night cruising.

Left: This '31 Ford coupe in bare metal has been given a maximum top chop, and it must be a bit of a problem for the driver to look out through those mail-slot windows, but it sure looks great.

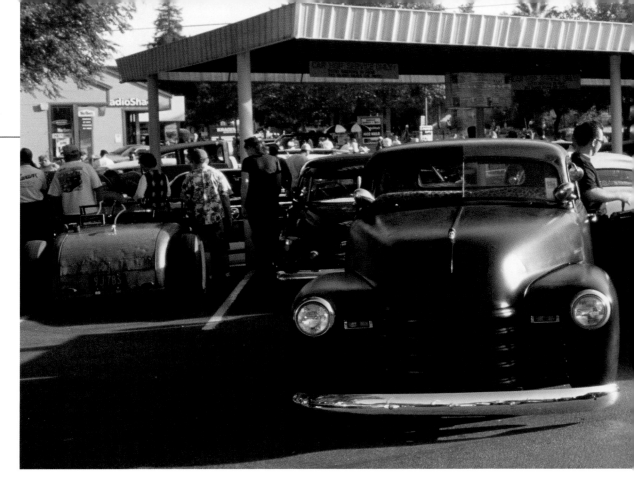

Right: Friday night is cruising night during the Paso Robles event, and many of the rockabilly boys use the A&W drive-in as their meeting spot. The parking lot is full of early style hot rods and customs, most of them in primer.

Below: You can see plenty of good-looking hot rods in Paso Robles, such as this black, five-window '32 coupe. It belongs to Darryl Spurlock from Modesto and has "Tommy the Greek" pinstriping to give it a little extra color.

Below: Bill Freni is featured in chapter 4 with his candy blue roadster, but he's just put this three-window coupe together with early hemi power. Rod builder Bill Brown did some of the work on the car. The flamed three-window in the background belongs to Buddy Dughi, who is also a member of the Lucky Devils.

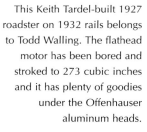
This Keith Tardel-built 1927 roadster on 1932 rails belongs to Todd Walling. The flathead motor has been bored and stroked to 273 cubic inches and it has plenty of goodies under the Offenhauser aluminum heads.

Jim "Bones" Notebom creates new customs every year, and this '39 Mercury coupe is one of his latest. The body has been smoothed out, and the chassis has been updated with air suspension and modern components along with a late model drivetrain.

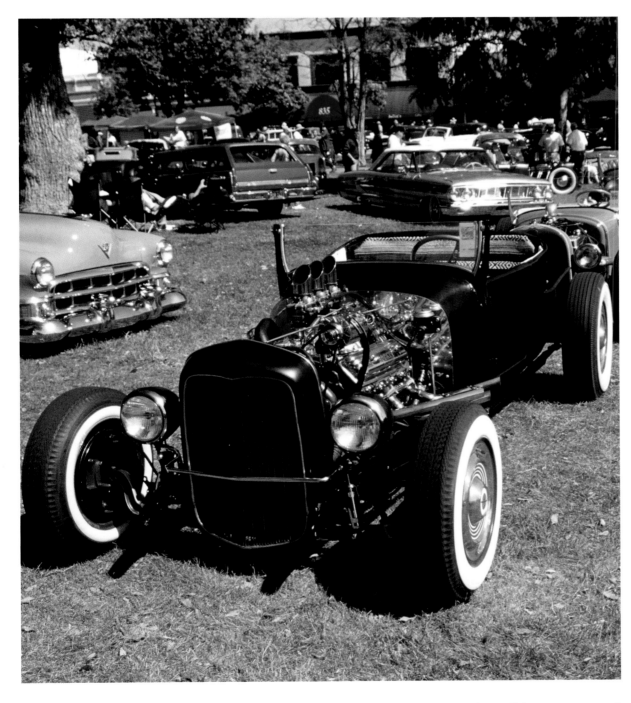

A row of early style hot rods, all of them with 1927 T-pickup-body style. Olds Rocket and Buick Nailhead engines are among the favorites for rockabilly cars.

complete cars had prices that belonged more at Disneyland, but the smart buyers wait a week or two to call the seller. If the car is still for sale, the price might be much better.

At the L.A. Roadsters event you meet all the people in the business, so many come from all over the country to visit. All the well-known street rod companies with their latest products can be found. Roy Brizio showed off a line of his nice hot rods, among them Eric Clapton's new 1932 roadster and the just-restored Tom McMullen roadster. So-Cal Speed Shop had a big tent with all their products,